D1600897

THE CUMULUS EFFECT

THE CUMULUS EFFECT

for Liza

[signature]

2016

J. MAE BARIZO

Four Way Books
Tribeca

Copyright © 2015 J. Mae Barizo
No part of this book may be used or reproduced in any manner
without written permission except in the case of brief quotations embodied in
critical articles and reviews.

Please direct all inquiries to:
Editorial Office
Four Way Books
POB 535, Village Station
New York, NY 10014
www.fourwaybooks.com

Library of Congress Cataloging-in-Publication Data

Barizo, J. Mae.
[Poems. Selections]
The cumulus effect / J. Mae Barizo.
pages ; cm
ISBN 978-1-935536-64-2 (softcover : acid-free paper)
I. Title.
PS3602.A77542A6 2015
811'.6--dc23

2015006032

This book is manufactured in the United States of America and printed on
acid-free paper.

Four Way Books is a not-for-profit literary press. We are grateful for the assistance
we receive from individual donors, public arts agencies, and private foundations.

This publication is made possible with public funds from the National Endowment for the Arts

and from the New York State Council on the Arts, a state agency

and from the Jerome Foundation.

[clmp]

We are a proud member of the Community of Literary Magazines and Presses.

Distributed by University Press of New England
One Court Street, Lebanon, NH 03766

"In 1596 Matteo Ricci taught the Chinese how to build a memory palace. He told them that the size of the palace would depend on how much they wanted to remember…"

The Memory Palace of Matteo Ricci, Jonathan D. Spence

Traum: German for **dream**.
Traum, from the Greek word, τραυμα, **a wound**.
In its verb form τιτρωσκω, **I injure**.

CONTENTS

THE CUMULUS EFFECT

I.

Thinking of you
I prick my smallest finger.

Pink sky.
Perhaps it will not stay.

Perhaps he is unfaithful
in this poem.

Each day I think
that he may die.

Pink sky! You are
too large for me to carry you

II.

It looks as if—
grey sky.

Cannot sleep,
frail leaf.

Dream: we rent
two movies in Italian.

Did he touch you?
On the eyebrows, in a ship.

III.

There are so many items
to pack in my valise.

Rows of
windy days?

A procession of
chariots rolling by?

Mustaches
of old men?

Are they clouds,
or sea?

IV.

In the text message:
a little bee.

I read your absence
like a novel

night it
seemed to me

was but an
autumn sonata

so loud I
could not sleep

V.

Perhaps she is unfaithful
in this poem.

Pray, my
restless

that such longing
will undo

the trees, all
dressed in nectarine

VI.

on the wind
a sentence

like an ochre
bee divine—

sorry I could
not carry you
in my mind.

NEW YORK

A hindsight of blood. The sill
with its speck of ash: who smoked
there? Tea on the lip as

a forgetting of another endeavor.
Red: aligning quietly on the eaves
or beneath the skin: *articulate, articulate.*

The dream of the wheel, bird
sounds, red of the hip like a
wrist corsage.

Snow under the hand, a different kind of muteness.
Something you once belonged to, the lines smudged.

In the other memory the severed arm speaks.
In the other memory it is as silent as snow.

In the transient form
everything subject to question.

A tilt, a bruise.

Later on, the killing time.

To outgrow your own hand
you must stop clasping.

Held in the clock's sway
the hand becomes tired
of so much secrecy.

Sooner or later
the hand will be
nowhere to be found.

Arm: a diamond. Nothing
at all to add to such flesh.
Mouth beautiful only when speaking
though a word may rip on the tongue like salt.

At the edge of an aisle
a cut of cold air on the thigh.
One child learns to whistle, the other
turns her eyelid inside out. Remembering
as a type of expiration. The hour itself that closes down.

She wakes to a box
full of bees.

Her childhood, suddenly smaller.

Next to your eye, a door.
Next to your door, a vestibule.
Next to your vestibule, it opens.

Now give me your mouth—

In the study of distance
everything meets the eye
as pool blue.

A cool light, undecided, comes
over the city.

The cloudswift sky unbuttons.

Everything remembers everything.

BERLIN

BERLIN

Eye which was a blindspot, snow bright.

The window, then. September already and the window he hauls
her bandaged wrist, fitting it with a white dress. *There we go,* he says
and tungsten is an element, no. 74, steely-gray and robust. The highest
melting point of all non-alloyed metals and in her eye some trace
of the colour. Its pure form. Tenderness, another form of despair.

Because everything that was said was a blade edge. Somewhere the night
turned down its leaves on the season, amethyst or indigo in its veins,
the two-fisted foliage. Trees so fastidious about their beauty, still green.
The lights winking in Senefelderplatz. Down the alleyway someone
was walking towards or turning away, a monochrome grace.

Not sleeping, not able even to sleep nor
toss with dreams nor *breath* nor *next to*.
Beyond the walls a belt of blue clouds
and afterwards another colour and all of this
before morning sound, too many trains.

Blue as in corridor. The motor of the day ground down beneath
the foot as in Beethoven, no earth sounds. How tardy always, how
sought after, desire [like a ribbon] wedded to the heel, pulling fast
when lids fall. Morning was but a code for leaving and taking, taking
and leaving. Blue like blood or *guard me from it*, cloud-light.

That daylight may be an imaginary opening. A yellow-hooded sweatshirt to live in so the body becomes a stem, petals lost to frenzy. This and the other occlusions. The pinhole of a word and what empties into it. Yellow like the pollen of a mouth.

Wire mesh, poplar, that strange dance.
Body by which to bend must move so
delicately like a dull minuet. And you
were magnetic field, voltage against
the eye of sun and bones that grated
one against the other. O motor
of my limbs, coiling through
the monotone days. How young then,
guarding me against every ruinous thing.

The time zone the dream was in, continual comings and goings, grass pressed down. How many times with or without she walked that green path. Lamp ash already, some days she knew and others she did not know and that outlasted any other music. Light came too slow to write it: street sounds, train sounds, the nowhereness of flight. In another city a phone was ringing, night walking away from morning, such faultlessness.

SAINT PETERSBURG
(THE MARBLE PALACE)

In the dream the season.
Water on the lash then farther down.
We kept hinged for the most part in an uneasy
crowd. Blue undiluted, no leaf cover.

There were people who remembered but mostly
boyish: the collection of objects as a method of—

(I was walking into the marble palace, tumblers full
of vodka, we lolled about an hour)

—*forgetting*. A hothouse, ellipsis.

Someone there was shaking my hand.

The memory then: *Milk breath, milk breath give me your hand.*
Names they had called her, bad kisses from a boy.

How do you do. Like the queen of the higher parallels
where the nights are always white, the season incessantly
        surprising us.   A prank e-mail from a Viennese friend:

If your heart is as bruised as your cunt, then what about it? There are
        thirty-two types of marble. There are treacheries that breach
even stone. Blue like vein. Grey like *armor me with.*

I wanted to be wearing beautiful shoes.
I wanted to say the word *profiterole.*

There was music coming from the inner yard.

Because there exists always a moment when one can say
how not to. Not to melt like gooseflesh, not to disappear
like a wife, how not *to build*. O skin rough-grained
as Finnish granite, polished pink Karelian of pilasters,
white Ural marble for your capitals and festoons!

Why breathe. One might break something. A late-night
                                     concert, a sonata
known by heart. The temporary
        flight from then to now. Sound taking
the space and the shape of

Someone was mouthing the word *quince.*
I was staring at the shock yellow of his hair.

Not that there can be an excuse for not speaking. The first winter
for example, when the Neva rose up like a wall of unintentioned
sound. Between the palace and the quay. Something erupting
like a midnight flower, a mouth or an artery or some type of.
Names thrown like javelins into the blood stream, an entire room
usurped by light. Her mind was a palimpsest: written on, scraped
off, scrawled over, again and again. She craved filthy cinemas
and foreign films. Sidewalks and shadow as it struck them.

What was written was meant to be forgotten: *Sometimes*
I sing so pretty it breaks my own heart.

With Mitya and Marthe, walking beside the river.

Let's start again: the blue watch
      and the slender wrist, line
      of low sky above the river. Journey as
voice to the back of the head. *Tra la la*

la la. A blur of wing. A ring from another
city. A street too hot for breathing.
                    A kiss
at the elbow makes a sound like

      Too much to remember. Was it
morning already? Which moment?
The moment of the threshold which
is almost not felt

The white wall, the white bed. The bright, empty
hall of her head

In the dream a voice said: Don't you wish to enter?
The womb, the calm vein, the palace of Konstantin Konstantinovich?
Come, hither

How swiftly we walked then, from the embankment to the Field of Mars;
Mitya talking vodka, Marthe farting from her nose.
             The boyish, for example, with his blonde
girls at the Griboedova club, the lapel-pin tremor of my pulse
pressed frenzy. *Where do you go, Madame, in your grey capuchon?*

The heart is a harem without the halogen lights. Painful
to look into, blurred by desire. Inside the desire
was like sleeping with barbed wires.

That was the beauty and the brunt of it: dreaming always
        on the pointed edge of wakefulness. Looking at your face
peering at an edifice so lovely.

And so it was that all she had construed in her mind
as ultimatum was rather a method by which to remain
among the living.

(The gates, for instance, in all their brilliance
not unlike the gaping of a mouth)

Not far off an opening.

A sonata was playing in the inner yard.

The heart was a radiant thing, in love
        with the word *profiterole.*

How swift I walked towards it.

AFRIKA

In the other country. The prehistoric one
         where what was given was what
was gone. A state where every sovereign
snagged what we held down. Green like
                          flesh when
full of wander and of wine. What was it
you said to me?

The land is the colour of cough drops. That
the earth is what we'd eat of when we died.

The citizens here are like watermarks, I said.
A stain or leaving no trace of.
Which are you.

Pick one.

How careful.

Years ago, a phone call across the Nile
and the flaccid voice, careless around the edges.

No, beautiful is your. . .

A crackling or a flame-wick and then
none. She turned back, teased a pant leg.

The backward glance, light blown into acacia trees.

Who is talking. The night-walkers perhaps
with their thin wrists and tapping sticks. On
the verdigris a slightly discernible halo of blood.

The cocktail party. *My name is
my name is my name is.*

Zabaglione, someone is
saying.

The cognac-coloured shoulder that
struck you like a drug.

Da da da da. A four-bar bit of Rachmaninoff looped
so it would repeat indefinitely.

                                           My name! I screamed
and your mouth swung open.

My inkstain.

There was a cacophony of pencils, Zulu masks, fur pressed down.
Somewhere down the stairs there was a ghost that hummed.

Scylla. You said. Between Scylla and Charybdis. That which
does not allow the sagging cliff of lust. Music? Allowed.
Mbira in Shona, *sanza, kalimba, likembe*
in other languages. *Thumb piano* in English.

An anorexic cat stood between us.

Ararat!

My mind was almost won.

In one instant he would be a locust, leaping for my mouth.

But he didn't know which way she'd like to be taken: the sun
so bright it's slapping her, bent forward like the barrel of a gun.

Marula tree liquor, someone else's cigarettes—objects
a distraction for the task at hand, her tongue against a thumb.

By the palace later, a wraith-like light.

Grey nights!

Grey night, a porcelain bird flung far across the waters,

the path implied.

Some days the river will whistle. *Hoo, hoo, hoo.* Looking for my face we peer inside but it is only palace trash. A chicken wing. Piss-blood.

He has on a velvet overcoat, capillary blue or slate like day or maybe when the light crawls by we'll look inside.

Rivers that are never blue.
It is not I.   It is not true.

And I was on my way soon, to Spreeuwen or Landestrasse, so many shifts of sun.

A postcard home, no details, just a square of childish writing.

> Anti-nostalgia: a whiff of skin
> like land-sight, the urge to pilfer
> rather than preserve.

And if there were no country (the last sentence only, when he is kneeling
at her chest) there would be no memory, neither an others or one's own.

How quick then, the mouth. And they were a solemn people: naming
the world, mapping it out, arguing about what it meant. Clandestine as

husbands, lamp-crash in the blood. So much to forget still. Wasn't there
dawn-light already? Kissing sounds on the back of a hand, river smell.

How swift the city, how hot the globe.

Press your ear against the shoreline, my restless,
and let us love warily, remembering nothing.

TRAUM

Red of cartwheels. First blood, pin-prick on a thumb. Otherwise known as *ashamed, forced into its last bastions.* AM radio, string quartet sound. As a child it was *husband,* the bridal dream; something that needed to be found. And it was futile then to escape out of the inner yard.

Skin as boundary of the subject. The eye the organ that distorts. In dream a tall flame snaked through the wide corridor. Leonine. As graceful as a drug.

A motion made to bridge the space inside the mind. Your arm across the eye, a blot against the sun. And the engine burping still, its tenacious hum. *Amfortas! Die Wunde! Die Wunde! Sie brennt mir hier zur Seite!*

Wound: it bloomed because the outside world talked back. Insolent,
dazed because the word was not enough. Later it would be *Mother*:
the urge to be cradled, lulled away from. Because the wound
was a kaleidoscope, shying away from sun.

(

I yearned, yes. I yearned. Art which was confession. Art which
was castor bean, an emetic against the hissing of the street, clothed
in phosphorescent light. And if you were to speak the sound would
echo not unlike the empty of a drum. Skin was but a detour to sleeping
and waking, waking and sleeping. Red like the thunder of your mouth.

And somewhere it splits. Armorless Parsifal, susceptible to falling. And secrets also, exposed by slight of skin or slip of tongue. There are scars there, undecipherable maps. The arsenal of touch.

Mother. Calling her by her maiden name, scarlet as an intestine. A wound which exudes rancor, static sound, no pianos. In the dream she comes to you so docile; supine, palms open and barbarous. When the music begins everything stays the same. When I look back again she is gone.

Final signs of civilization: Cloying, trashy, like ketchup.
The horizon a farther wall, shut off like the radio. Blood, blood,
thanatos and in the mind a fugue careening through the blight.
The spear then. The spear *Amfortas, your war is almost won!*
It is but a dream *Say it again* but a dream. Dazed, you looked
so long but it is lacquered already. No earth sounds.

When you woke there was music still. Scissored melodies, nameable
to none. Light because dream was indistinguishable as skin against
skin. The colour only, existing as a pink streak against the cheek.
When I returned to you it was as if all was healed: absence of noise.
Behaving in the dawn light as opera at the curtain call, all else forgotten.
It bled between the fingers, the memory of what we longed for.
And the music still. And the sun.

NOTES

The title "The Cumulus Effect" was first seen in a *New York Times* article (October 8, 2006) by Herbert Muschamp describing an architectural trend for constructing buildings that resemble clouds, "condensations of social space."

The section "Saint Petersburg," was originally entitled "The Marble Palace." The palace was commissioned by Catherine the Great for a favourite count, Grigory Orlov.

The poem "TRAUM" owes a debt to the exhibition "Traum and Trauma" at Kunsthalle Vienna. Further readings include the essay "Art and Wound, the Aesthetics of Dream and Trauma" by Angela Stief and Gerald Matt. German text in "TRAUM" is from *Parsifal* by Wolfram Von Eschenbach. *Amfortas! Die Wunde! Die Wunde! Sie brennt mir hier zur Seite!* translates to "The wound! The wound! It burns here in my side."

ACKNOWLEDGMENTS

Grateful acknowledgment is made to *AGNI Online, Boxcar Poetry Review, Eleven Eleven,* and *Sink Review* where versions of these poems first appeared.

Thank you to Daniel and Ophelia Barizo, Wolfram and Ada Koessel, Amanda Barizo and Elizabeth Lanning, Richard Scheiwe, Askold Melnyczuk, Sven Birkerts, Amy Gerstler, Timothy Liu, Major Jackson, Ed Ochester, Jean Valentine, David Daniel, Anne Wenzel, Dmitry Golynko, Darren Bifford, Rob Moose, and Vikram Rajan.

Born in Toronto, J. Mae Barizo is a poet, critic, and performer. Recent work appears in *AGNI*, *Bookforum*, *Boston Review*, and *Los Angeles Review of Books*. She is the recipient of fellowships and awards from Bennington College, the Jerome Foundation, and Poets House. A classically-trained musician and advocate of cross genre collaboration, she lives in New York City.